I0231377

SPOOL IN THE MAZE

SPOOL IN THE MAZE

COLLEEN O'BRIEN

NEW MICHIGAN PRESS
TUCSON, ARIZONA

NEW MICHIGAN PRESS
DEPT OF ENGLISH, P. O. BOX 210067
UNIVERSITY OF ARIZONA
TUCSON, AZ 85721-0067

<http://newmichiganpress.com>

Orders and queries to nmp@thediagram.com.

Copyright © 2015 by Colleen O'Brien.
All rights reserved.

ISBN 978-1-934832-48-6. FIRST PRINTING.

Printed in the United States of America.

Design by Ander Monson.

Cover image © Laura Mackin, *Internet Mirrors (Forest No. 11)*, 2013, C-print, 20 × 20 inches

CONTENTS

For B

REEL

A reel is a dance,
a spool,
and a fall fast and straight
at the wall.

To reel and to fall make a cross
like to rise and to sail.
To bow makes a compass
to draw on the floor.

A draw is a truce.
The fall ends the year.
A headstone's a tooth
in the mouth of the earth.

Truth is a word
in the mouth
and a spool in the maze
in the myth.

ERGO EGO

all ends and
I am profoundly
I can bear to say
unafraid of death
this only
because I do not
believe in death
in other languages certainly not
in my own

PLATO'S METAPHORS

When he spoke
about Lachesis, Clotho, Atropos

when he spoke of them as women

at a loom—not three points defining
an infinite plane, slicing any thing,

man, monument, mountain, the sun,

not wall, nor floor, nor constellation—

when he,
before solid geometry,

before space-time, believed in *is,*

and still incarnated in air the women
turning whorls studded with planets, was he

condescending
even to his spiritual sons—or had he come in fact

to ecstasy, to a region

where reason's heat
passes blue and

shatters into gods?

CITY LANDSCAPE

After Joan Mitchell

It told her what to do,
the gorged-on-color mouth
between white planes, as if

all were mouth beneath.
All sound: a throng
of foreign tongues

in which she thought
she heard her name ring out.
One neural region all alight

inside skull dark,
the needed seal
that told her what to do

(and weather scored the sky like claws
and worms escaped into the soil):
it told her *drown me out.*

WIND TURNS RAIN

wind turns rain and all
        shatters lightly

        but does
not separate

a dripping geometric
        darkness lids

        the moving view

        we are going
        closer farther

MOLLY

o rocks! fat un

          faithful
Penny in rank
bedsheets, reading dirty books to ferry all

ye blaze, ye boil
          ing souls over the white fat foaming

oash, one waving
          luscious arm, bare from her

window, seen
by whom? that scrap

          of morning

mail, the privy under bed
          awaiting her

Hellenic stream,
          her instrument

beneath, untuned
                    piano where she ulu

lates, undoes
            the day's loom

work again,
            again she says,

            against
the soldier's youth

ful wall,
            and da, and da

rkness lit by moon, all
moonsday, met him

            wild
centrifuge rose

            en bloom.

FUEL

And I am the downed tree
and the thriving sorrel,

the calcite logarithmic spiral
shell, and the gum creature

oozing and perishing inside.
My live corpse feeds

the frothing ever breeding;
my multiplying

petrifies.

RUINED LION

Mane of moss,
maw simplified to toothless
shrunken gums. Demoted
to a phylum worse, some white-eyed
sucking worm. His mother
burst with none to nurse, she's melted
to her throne. Has crying done
that to her face? What turns
stone to loam?

MIDAS

I sit here in ass's ears
through which no human
language passes,

only the four-tone scale
of all mammalia: relief
and coming relief, pain

and coming pain. The notes
sound nearly always
in isolation,

occasionally in ligated
but still distinct dyads.
Every hour I forget

more of the sapiens
mouth, even its ordinary
virtuosity,

and every hour I am
more afraid to speak.

CONSOLATION TO A FRIEND

You had more talent than he did.
His luck came younger.
World knows the way that goes:
luck, hunger, and luck-hunger.

Or was the difference inside?
One must have a mind of summer
to get the grapes the rest of us
are jumping under,

which obviously are ripe,
but won't fill one forever.

JUDITH BUTLER

through the many mattresses she
felt the tiny, adamant pea

and couldn't sleep

and picked a thread,
another thread, tore up

a boll
of fluffy stuff,

tempest
of feathers and frivolité,

of knotted lace,
the shuttles mummying

stout thread, she found
the cache of silicone

and wrinkled dugs
and dug

on down—confessed
(they begged) it's just

a little better for the man—

and when
she had it in her hand,

that dived-for bit
of oyster grit,

the mattresses a shameless
mess,

she slid it neatly in
her ring

and went to wake
the castle up.

BECAUSE WE WANT

it there, we put
it there

our wanting it
is it
   it is

            father
            lover
lastly
            genre

please
here,
a variation on refrain

            (smell of sex,
            drinking
            with children in the house)

because we put it there

            (how we
            all stayed friends)

every borrowing

drags along with it
          the whole

we put it there because

please here

WHAT IS THIS

What is this
"William Carlos Williams"

that makes
me feel

a secret peer

like my private
chaste sensuousness

is rare

William borne by
Williams plural,

as if all come
in him

to one and

then that
audacious careless

Latinate flourish
plash center—

this other than

man or
pen manned

THE AFTER-MAN

wants ~~an art that~~

a that which

exceeds ~~calculation and~~

wants

~~abrogation of~~
a that with which

to reset
~~the hands of the~~

the heads of the
clock

wants

at zero

a clock which

wants

to reset
with

hands ~~which~~
but

breaking with the past [strikethru]

is actually ~~forgetting~~

repeating

the ~~sublime is~~
that which

~~is wanted~~ exceeds

breaking

ON DRAWING MARCUS AURELIUS

Take hold
of the horse, its neck
and bulging eye.
Then learn the man
by head. Be him,
be unsurprised.

Take hold
of the thing described.
His cockleshell
beard, his size
astride that burly
beast not even
slightly compromised.

Forget verisimilitude.
Be alloyed,
streaked with green
and gold. Solid as
an earth-packed
age. Solemn
as bronze.

BATHERS BY A RIVER

After Matisse

I

Here, in the breath white
light the long necked
girl, from a moment

when logic, form,
and organ met—
supple reaching neck—

and eye confirmed
what mind prescribed.

II

Black gravity
and gray vibration:
Electrons or
their likelihood.

Green where his mind changed.
Previous green in
simultaneous pink.

III

Reeds row up
like tusks.
Eight years
for a long moment.

Given the chance
he'd change it.
Reeds pile like Sunday palms
on the moment.

IV

He found her body
at last like a tree
in the reeds.
Blackline growth
up the cloven legs
and buttocks

as in that miniature
Cezanne he called moral,
black wet locks
coiled like proteins.

IN THE DEMOCRACY

My father went to the mirror
every morning half naked
and scraped cream
from his beard. He flexed
both biceps, blue
plastic razor puny
in his fist. His face
half cream, half red
and clean, he made
a beast-face to make
me shriek laughing.
He believed
that he was joking.

FOR NOW

the infant's eyes' unheimlich
automatic motion

open asleep in the foremilk
of human cognition,

in blank concatenation:
rampant rebus minus

meaning: a color-
shallow surface

blindly doubling
the ceiling

fan blades' turning

AMERICA WINDOWS

After Chagall

Fall under
the white-gloved hornblower,
    goldheaded in lightfall splintered
        from organ pipes'

glister, fall
with white eye-leaves under
    the blue viola, raise
    your roundend nose
        to the shameless

deepening, to fisheyed
    shadows rushing over
        dusk-shut shop

windows, hold
    the viola's bow,
        hold
    the yellow-eyed moon
    white wingeating sun over

morning again, the wet
        bridges—

and she
swarmed in sinuate leaves for the late
  ballet—and he still new
    born, a boy

uncullled behind
    these spiral doors.

BRIDGE

After Joseph Stella

This bridge—I
came here painfully
young. What did I
do at a blue stoplight?
I wished for that light
to mean I was
asleep. To know
I slept and marvel
at that least
illumination.
Cathedral
window bridge;
the frame backlit
and black. All that
apparatus—necessary—
layered on the air.

MODERN WING

Whether the letters of an unread headline
Whether the newt-rabbit, blue and virile
Whether sketched or sculpted, the thorn extractor
Who competes with the stick-trained geranium,

The woman is the wallpaper
The woman is the stuffed cushion
The large-eared decorative housecat
Is the house's bathing heart.

ONLY IS THERE

only is there

y : cloud of phonemes/signifying bits

        speaking a tissue

x christens
sense

        emitting sound

of which *x* is
feedback

only

totality
in the (*x*-christening)

of direction toward

totality not
there.

This is true: I once overheard

this lie:

naranja is equivalent *n'orange*
and thus

grazing the hurdle is

not orange.

THE INTERPRETATION OF DREAMS

All the stage is
bearded like a pard, is

justice in her.

All the quarrel, satchel,
hose with eyes

severe.

A ballad to her.

All the wide is
creeping like her

beard of formal
cut,

the cannon's mouth,

sans teeth.

Big manly pard, sudden
like furnace his

big manly
ballad.

    Eyebrow.

His shrunk.

Last strange of
all a world

too wide.

CHILD IS FATHER

We are farther post-Christian and richer entropic,
make more of our movements and less of our masses.

We matter as physics. Our matter's less ethics.
Without them we're moral as moons and we orbit

no center. We make a mathematics
that roots in a stillness less stable than zero.

We matter as ether, no-telos our telos,
and stake your ascendance with flags of our absence.

SATURN

Red throat,
expel today
the substitute:
the stone. The boy

is back from
underground
today. The boy
has grown.

The undigested
breach in yellow
glory from my
mouth. Then blast

me nine days'
anvil flight away
from wide-
wayed earth.

BLAUE REITER SONG

Give me the soaring Roman viaduct,
rock face and yellow wall,
the stilt man with his trombone,
and the royal's jellied poule;

Make me the red calf in the cataract,
the blue-black ass and pool,
and white froth out the steel flue
of the hot-wheeled witching mill.

OLD NOTES

rereading old notes I take
a semicolon for a lowercase *i*

; confuse *i*
with a kind

of notational fulcrum ; take
a hybrid

a stacked
stop and go

for a kind
of notational fiction

[stop stop] many centuries'
pondering [stop stop]

"note thinks therefore
note is" [stop go]

then typing drop
the *e* on *note*

"not thinks therefore . . ."

it's not
like *me* to lowercase

whimsically [stop go] it's not
like me to game italics, splash

[quote quote] and such

about, say *o*

paren
but then,
what *is* it like?

look at me [go]

THOSE ARE PEARLS

Row row row your boat, gently down the stream your
boat, merrily merrily mer your boat: Life is but a
dream your boat

Row row rowily merrily: Life is but the stream your
boat, Rowily rowily rowily merrily: Life is but a
row your boat

Gently down the stream your boat, gentilly downily
row your boat, gently but the stream your boat:
Life is merrily merrily merrily

Row is but a dream your boatily, gently but a row
your boatily, row is merrily dream your boatily,
merrily but a merrily boatily

Merrily but a dream your boat, merrily down the
stream your merrily, Gently but a merrily merrily,
Life is merrily dream your boat

Life is but a dream your boat: Life is but the stream
your boat: Life is down the stream your boat:
Gently but the stream your boat

Gently down the stream your merrily, Row row row
your merrily, Gently down the streamily merrily,
Row is but a row your merrily

Merrily merrily merrily merrily, merrily merrily
merrily merrily, merrily merrily merrily merrily,
merrily merrily merrily merrily

ACKNOWLEDGMENTS

I want to thank Richard Kenney for being a very good teacher. Also Olivia Friedman and Zac Cotler, for challenging and encouraging my poetry early on, and Mike Rutherglen, Glenn Shaheen, Elizabyth Hiscox, Douglas Jones, Scott Bade, and Nancy Eimers for careful, honest readings of many of these poems. Brandon Krieg, for all of the above, among other things.

Many thanks also to the editors of the following publications, where some of the poems were first published:

Another Chicago Magazine: "Bathers by a River"
Beloit Poetry Journal: "Plato's Metaphors," "Fuel," "Child Is Father," "Because We Want," "The After-Man"
CutBank: "On Drawing Marcus Aurelius," "In the Democracy"
Denver Quarterly: "For Now"
DIAGRAM: "America Windows"
Kenyon Review Online: "The Interpretation of Dreams"
The Journal: "Reel," "Ruined Lion," "Modern Wing" (published as "Matisse")
Poetry Northwest: "Consolation to a Friend"
West Branch: "Midas"
Witness: "Bridge," "Saturn"

COLLEEN O'BRIEN was born in 1979 and grew up in Chicago. She received a BA from Stanford University and an MFA from the University of Washington. Her fiction and poetry have appeared in *The Antioch Review*, *North American Review*, *Kenyon Review Online*, *Ninth Letter*, *Witness*, and other publications. She is currently a PHD student at Western Michigan University.

COLOPHON

Text is set in a digital version of Jenson, designed by Robert Slimbach in 1996, and based on the work of punchcutter, printer, and publisher Nicolas Jenson. The titles are in Futura.

NEW MICHIGAN PRESS, based in Tucson, Arizona, prints poetry and prose chapbooks, especially work that transcends traditional genre. Together with *DIAGRAM*, NMP sponsors a yearly chapbook competition.

DIAGRAM, a journal of text, art, and schematic, is published bimonthly at THEDIAGRAM.COM. Periodic print anthologies are available from the New Michigan Press at NEWMICHIGANPRESS.COM.

www.ingramcontent.com/pod-product-compliance
Lightning Source LLC
Chambersburg PA
CBHW031503040426
42444CB00007B/1194
* 9 7 8 1 9 3 4 8 3 2 4 8 6 *